# Make Me an Instrument of Thy Peace

# Make Me an Instrument of Thy Peace

✦

*Lessons for Today from St. Francis of Assisi*

*Dr. Charles E. Smith*

iUniverse, Inc.
New York  Lincoln  Shanghai

# Make Me an Instrument of Thy Peace
## *Lessons for Today from St. Francis of Assisi*

iUniverse, Inc.

For information address:
iUniverse, Inc.
2021 Pine Lake Road, Suite 100
Lincoln, NE 68512
www.iuniverse.com

ISBN: 0-595-27939-2

Printed in the United States of America

This book is dedicated to individuals of all races, religions, and cultures who hear and respond to the voice of God calling them to the vocation of peacemaker.

# *Contents*

# INTRODUCTION

o o o o o o o o o o o o o o o o o o o o o o o o o o o o o o o o o o o

*"Lord, make me an instrument of Your peace, Where there is hatred let me sow love; where there is injury, pardon; where there is doubt, faith; where there is despair, hope; where there is darkness, light; and where there is sadness, joy."*

Apart from the Lord's Prayer and the Serenity Prayer, the Prayer of St. Francis is, perhaps, the most recognized and appreciated prayer in all of religious literature.

Events of September 11, 2001, brought attention of the world to bear on the need for peace. *Make Me An Instrument of Thy Peace* brings to light the timeless teachings of St. Francis as solutions for today's trouble world by focusing on human conditions that cause conflict, strife, and violence applying to each the remedy for peace proposed by St. Francis.

◆         ◆         ◆

St. Francis was born in 1181 or 1182 in the town of Assisi overlooking the Tiber River as it makes it way toward Rome and the Mediterranean Sea.

The name given him at his baptism was Giovanni, but early on he acquired the nickname "Francis," the name by which he is best known.

Ardent, charming, and sensitive, as a young man Francis was something of a playboy. His transition from a life of revelry to one of religion was gradual, prompted in part by illnesses and disappointments encountered during adolescence.

When Francis began spending more and more time in solitude in the fields surrounding Assisi and in service to the poor and lepers, behavior thought strange by his fellow townsmen, his father, Pietro Bernardeno took his son before the bishop with thoughts of disinheriting him.

Stripping himself of the clothing provided by his father, Francis declared his desire to serve God.

It was while listening to prayers in 1209 that Francis heard the voice of God calling him into service.

He became a wandering preacher calling men to repentance, living on whatever food was given him.

In time Francis began attracting others who felt as he did. Those who joined him he compelled to sell their goods, give the proceeds to the poor, and like the disciples Jesus appointed to go ahead of Himself in Luke 10:10-24, to go about their ministry taking neither staff, food, money, nor second coat with them.

In their preaching the Brothers of St. Francis stressed adoration of God, repentance, generosity, and the forgiveness of wrongs. They made much of love for one's neighbors and enemies, humility, and abstinence from vices.

In 1210, Francis and his companions went to Rome seeking permission of Pope Innocent III to pursue their way of life.

In time the Penitents of Assisi as they were known, became an order.

In 1126, while still in his forties, having lived the full life of a servant, Francis died. Two years later he was elevated to sainthood.

◆     ◆     ◆

Several features make this book unique and beneficial reading.

It takes a studied look at the prayer of St. Francis and its relevance for bringing peace to a troubled world by identifying human conditions that make for conflict, strife and violence and applying to each the remedy for peace proposed by St. Francis.

In this regard love is the remedy for hate, pardon for injury, faith for doubt, hope for despair, light for darkness, and joy for sadness.

Recognizing people the world over are connected by the bond of humanity it challenges everyone us to become involved in working for peace.

Thirdly, it demonstrates the paradox of those who work for peace, namely, that in consoling others we are consoled, in understanding others we are understood, in loving others we are loved, in giving to others we receive, in pardoning others we are pardoned, and in dying we are born to eternal life.

# 1

# *MAKE ME AN INSTRUMENT OF THY PEACE*

o o o o o o o o o o o o o o o o o o o o o o o o o o o o o o o o o o
*"Let there be peace on earth and let it begin with me."*

Some years ago, while traveling through the American southwest, I drove to the summit of Pike's Peak from where it is said Katharine Lee Bates was inspired to write *"America the Beautiful."*

Somehow, having been there, I cannot help but think that inspiration for writing the song many feel should be our national anthem could well be attributed to the peace experienced in that place as to the view Katherine Bates had of spacious skies, amber waves of grain, and the majesty of purple mountains above fruited plains.

◆          ◆          ◆

In the days preceding the Passover feast Jesus and the disciples set out on what was to be His last visit to the city of Jerusalem.

Aware His days on earth are numbered and His ministry nearing an end, Jesus begins preparing His disciples for what He knew awaited him in the city.

Knowing His words will create fear and apprehension in men with whom He has a close, tender, and open relationship, has taught when they needed guidance and direction, and counseled when they were confused and puzzled, Jesus moves to comfort them.

*"Peace I leave with you"* He says, *"My peace I give unto you."* (RSV)

◆      ◆      ◆

In contrast with other symbols Jesus used to awaken a sense of the presence of God in men, peace was a symbol with which the disciples were acquainted because of their understanding of Jewish scriptures in which peace was essentially personal and social well being, or "shalom."

Furthermore, from ancient times it had been the practice among Jews to invoke blessings of shalom when encountering or taking leave of each other.

By means of such blessings, Jews said to each other, "I wish you peace, everything that contributes to contentment, works to your good, and contributes to your well-being, everything that promotes tranquility and order in your life, including your relationships."

Because Jesus' disciples were Jews, in all likelihood they used blessings of shalom to communicate their wishes and intentions toward one.

Pronouncing a blessing upon homes that received them was one of the first things travelers did upon securing lodging for the night.

When Jesus sent disciples on a preaching mission in Matthew 10:5-16, He instructed them to pronounce blessings of peace upon homes that received them. As people of the time believed blessings contained the power to bring them to reality, hosts had reason to be elated when guests pronounced blessings upon their homes.

◆      ◆      ◆

Jesus spoke of peace using the Greek word "*eirana.*" He chose this word because it established His peace as inner peace, peace dependent upon God in contrast to peace as the world understands it, namely, a lessening of tension and conflict dependent upon the erection of structures and the creation of conditions to which the wills of men and nations can be bound.

In the same way the presence of the Lord accompanied the Children of Israel in a cloud by day and a pillar of fire by night in their exodus from Egypt, and the presence of the shepherd brought peace to sheep walking through the Valley of the Shadow of Death in the Shepherd's Psalm, the peace Jesus bestows upon men assures them of His presence even *"to the ends of the earth."*

◆        ◆        ◆

In the Beatitudes Jesus declared His desire to bless those who acquired traits and characteristics desired in disciples and citizens of the Kingdom of God. He did so knowing inner peace comes to those who detach from the world and all the world values and place their trust in God, as well as those who share their presence with neighbors when ties with persons emotionally significant to them are severed.

It comes as well to those who acquire the strength of character required to express anger without allowing anger to lead them to sin and those who show mercy and compassion to neighbors whose situations are difficult and whose circumstances are unfortunate.

Peace comes also to those filled with the righteousness of God and those upon whom the world visits trouble because their lives are so much like that of Christ that they cannot be ignored.

◆        ◆        ◆

Because men and nations have not comprehended the difference between the peace Jesus gives and peace as the world understands it, peacemaking has always been an arduous and difficult undertaking.

Certainly this has been the case in the Middle East, an area governed by ancient rivalries and conflicts where, in recent times at least, efforts at making peace have been largely a matter of attempting to erect structures and create conditions to which the wills of Jews and Palestinians could be bound.

While all efforts at peacemaking are to be applauded, regrettably history has demonstrated time and again that peace dependent upon external structures and conditions is susceptible to sabotage by men who would keep alive memories of ancient feuds and those who would remember sins and trespasses committed against them rather than forgive those who commit them.

But, most importantly, peace as the world understands it does not last because external structures and conditions do not build brotherhood without which peace is impossible.

◆     ◆     ◆

In light of conflicting understandings of peace, how are people in an aggressive, ambitious, success-driven society to become instruments of God's peace? What must they do to sow peace in the lives of others?

To be instruments of God's peace individuals must first believe they have been called from a self-centered and superficially expressed life to that of a servant of God.

It is the certainty that they have been called to a life of service that lends dignity and authenticity to the vocation of peacemaker, motivating those who work for peace to divest themselves of any trait, behavior, or characteristic that could render them less effective in sowing love, pardon, faith, hope, light, and joy in lives plagued by hatred, injury, doubt, despair, darkness, and sadness.

◆     ◆     ◆

To be effective instruments of God's peace individuals must be at peace with themselves as it is impossible to sow something in the life of others that is missing in one's own life.

At the core of our being is an area of spiritual and psychological significance called the "inner life." Here is housed the things we believe in. Here is decided how we are to live out what we believe. To experience peace these areas must be in harmony with each other. What we believe must square with how we live.

◆     ◆     ◆

To be effective in the task of peacemaking each person must fashion an image of themselves we can esteem and present in ways that encourage others to trust us.

As we see the world, people, and what happens to us in terms of who we are, a healthy self-image is essential if one is to succeed as a maker of peace.

In many ways the image we have of ourselves is the house we live in and self-esteem how much we like our house.

The greater the esteem one has for their self-image the more effective they are connecting with others as there is less in them to hinder sowing love, pardon, faith, hope, light, and joy while the lower the esteem an individual has for their image the less effective they are at sowing these virtues.

◆ ◆ ◆

F. W. Riggs raises an intriguing point when he suggests peace as a kind of war pitting love against hate, pardon against injury, faith against doubt, hope against despair, light against darkness, and joy against sadness.

Paul would have responded enthusiastically to the idea of peace as war against opponents that were not of flesh and blood armed with faith, hope, and love.

The value of faith as a weapon in a war of this kind lies in its capacity to convince people that peace in the core of one's being brings wholeness, tranquility, and order to life, while the value of hope lies in its capacity to keep alive a vision of what life might be like for people filled with wholeness and completeness, contentment and fulfillment.

And, while faith is the power, and hope, the vision needed to wage war successfully against injury, doubt, despair, darkness, and sadness, it is love that motivates instruments of God's peace to pray for and dialogue with individuals, organizations, and nations who foster conflict and thrive on fear, hate, violence, loneliness, hunger, and disorder.

◆ ◆ ◆

As "hate is strong," war against hate and fear is destined to be never-ending, fought on a variety of battlefields ranging from the human heart to the home.

While the enemy may not be flesh and blood, there is present in society and each one of us factors that make the task of the peacemaker difficult, but instruments of peace find satisfaction in the fact that the reward for bringing wholeness, contentment, and fulfillment to the lives of others is the honor of being called as "children of God."

◆ ◆ ◆

In light of recent events and conflicting understandings of peace, the prayer of St. Francis has become a model for all who work for peace.

One thing is certain, regardless of how loudly people of the world may condemn war, terrorism, and violence, neither arms nor weapons, structures or conditions bring lasting inner peace.

Inner peace finds men in the beauty of a sunset, the roar of a great river, in the movement of wind through the tress, the sleep of infants, the performance of great music, dance, and drama, and especially, in the selfless giving and the sacrifices men make that life might be better for those around them.

# 2

# *WHERE THERE IS HATRED LET ME SOW LOVE*

o o o o o o o o o o o o o o o o o o o o o o o o o o o o o o o o o

*"Though I speak with tongues of men and of angels and have diminished love, I am nothing."*

—*Adapted*

Having prayed the Lord make him an instrument of peace, St. Francis continued, *"Where there is hatred, let me sow love."*

Emotions of hatred and love are direct opposites, and while hatred is difficult to define and definitions of love are numerous, essentially, one is the antithesis of the other.

To psychologist Sven Wahlroos hatred is "a feeling of conscious enjoyment of another's misery or misfortune, a wish for him to be unhappy or hurt in some way."[1]

As emotions are energy and like snowballs rolling downhill grow and intensify, when hate is dwelt upon there is always a possibility that strife, conflict, and the use of force with the intent to harm will result.

It was Bertrand Russell who contended modern civilization made the human heart more prone to hatred than to friendship.

And it could be that the pace and demands of living in a post-modern society does separate men from each other, especially when one considers that with each technological advance opportunities for connecting in friendship diminish.

---

1.  Sven Wahlroos, *Family Communication* (New York: Macmillan Publishing Company, 1974), p. 250.

◆        ◆        ◆

Love has been described as that which distinguishes humankind from all other aspects of Creation, the medicine of moral evil, a gift, a thirst for communion, and the force that makes the world go around.

St. Francis' request to sow love may have been prompted by the knowledge that man's primary need is for relationship and awareness that when this need is not met man experiences a state of aloneness God saw in the Garden of Eden was not good because it prompts him to feel cut off or detached from, out of fellowship and communication with, unrelated to and, perhaps, unloved by other people.

Alone in any of these ways men are lonely because they feel deprived of emotionally satisfying relationships.

Casual observation confirms an alarming number of lonely people in society at the present time.

The primary explanation for so much loneliness seems to be that people have not been able to form meaningful relations with one another because the image they have of themselves is not one they can esteem and present effectively in their interactions with others.

Loneliness suggests an inability to establish relationships in which one's needs and those of society can be met and one's uniqueness is recognized and affirmed.

Unable to connect effectively with others, individuals tend to withdraw and isolate themselves or to establish and remain in unproductive relationships rather than risk having no relationships at all.

◆        ◆        ◆

Everyone carries a mental picture, image, or idea of who they are in their mind.

It would be difficult to overstate the importance of this image, because essentially, it is the frame of reference or lens through which we approach the world, others, and interpret what happens in our lives.

As such it is the key to one's personality, has a bearing upon everything we do, say, think, and feel, and is a factor in every relationship we establish, including our relationship with God.

It is important, however, to recognize

• some aspects of this image work for us, attract people to us, help build relationships, and ease communication between oneself and others

• that other aspects work against us, creating tension between ourselves and others, making communication more difficult, and

• as communication is largely non-verbal, that with every contact we have with others we communicate our self-image and how we feel about it without intentionally thinking about it.

◆     ◆     ◆

Esteem for the image we have of ourselves is an estimate of how important we are in our own eyes. It is an indication of how much we like, love, accept, and own the image we have of ourselves. In a sense self-esteem is the assessment we make of our worth, value, and significance.

To be effective in the task of peacemaking it is important that individuals see themselves as persons of worth and value, consider themselves their own best friend, and comfortable with the one person they cannot get away from no matter how hard they try, namely, themselves.

High self-esteem suggests people are pleased with themselves and are glad to be who they are, while low self-esteem suggests people are small in their own eyes.

◆     ◆     ◆

Interestingly enough while love is the principal doctrine of the Christian faith there are some within the Body of Christ for whom the idea of loving oneself smacks of egotism, self-centeredness, and pride.

This position must be challenged; on theological grounds because we are commanded to love ourselves; on psychological grounds because loving oneself is a sign of mental health, and on relational grounds because failure to love oneself makes it difficult to establish and maintain relationships with other people.

To feel that a positive, loving, and affirming attitude toward oneself runs counter to Christian doctrine disregards the fact that egotism and self-centeredness are signs of a poor relationship with oneself, in fact, states of aloneness characterized by fear.

The problem associated with egotism and self-centered people is not so much that they think more highly of themselves than they ought as it is that they are not convinced the things they say about themselves are true.

Therefore, the airs of the conceited, the displays associated with the egotistical, and the exaggerated calling attention to themselves characteristic of the self-centered must be seen for what they are, attempts on the part of people small in their own eyes to convince themselves that they are persons of worth and value.

◆      ◆      ◆

Individuals who perceive self-love as egotistical, self-centered, and prideful are quick to quote Paul's caution, *"Do not think more highly of yourself than you ought,"*(NIV) in support of their position.

While it is important to pay attention to what Scripture says, it is equally important to note what it does not say.

What Scripture does not say is that we are not to think highly of ourselves. Made in the image of God we have every right to love who we are because we are a part of God's Creation, in fact, its crowning touch, the only aspect of Creation crowned with the honor of reflecting the image of its Creator. Not to think highly of ourselves we demean the Creation God pronounced good.

Paul was not saying, "Don't think highly of yourselves," but rather, "Don't think more highly of yourself than you ought in matters of faith."

He issued this caution because some members of the congregation at Rome were elevating themselves above others and withholding fellowship on the basis of their understanding of the faith, offices held, and functions performed within the congregation.

What these individuals were overlooking was that the measure of faith one enjoys is a gift of God and has nothing to do with offices held or functions performed.

Because it is not good for man to be alone to himself, man has every right to think highly of himself, and be his own best friend and closest neighbor. Only then will he love his neighbor and his God as he is commanded.

◆      ◆      ◆

To facilitate the task of sowing love where hatred is present instruments of peace must develop the art of connecting with people in ways that encourage others to invite them into their lives.

# *Suggestions For Building Trust*

1. Trust exists when the basis for connecting is mutual confidence.

To connect with others in ways that encourage them to trust, individuals must trust themselves. If you don't trust yourself, it is highly unlikely others will find you trustworthy.

2. To merit trust, you must accept others without reservation.

Acceptance doesn't require that you like someone or condone anything they do.

It requires only that you respect others, listen to them, show interest in them, express appreciation for them, and acknowledge things that make them who they are, at the same time, withhold making judgments regarding these things.

3. Acknowledge factors in your experience, yourself, and society likely to inhibit the building of trust in relationships.

4. If there is some trait, characteristic, inclination, or tendency in you that makes it difficult for others to view you worthy of their trust, in the interest of greater effectiveness as an instrument of God's peace, change it.

5. Take the initiative in connecting with others. Be willing to share your thoughts, ideas, opinions, feelings, and experiences with others. Let them know how you feel about them and how their behavior affects you.

6. Become comfortable with the fact that not everyone is going to deem you worthy of trust.

When this happens, don't take offence. Take into account that the people whom you want to trust you are as fragile, faulted, and imperfect as yourself. Accept as well that their non-acceptance does not relieve you of the responsibility of modeling what is required for one person to trust another.

When people do not see you as worthy of their trust, learn from the experience and move on.

7. As everyone has what Abraham Maslow described as a hierarchy of needs, commit yourself to building trust by meeting the needs and acting in the best interests of those in whose lives you desire to sow the virtues Francis named in his prayer.

Meeting needs builds trust. Think of trust as a warm fuzzy you carry in a bag. If you will give your fuzzies away your bag will always be full, for trust like bread cast upon the waters returns in the form of acceptance.

8. Keep in mind that you have been called to something higher, greater, and purer than yourself, therefore, in the interest of sowing love refrain from introducing any form of distortion into relationships with others. Your only agenda is to sow love, pardon, faith, hope, light, and joy in the lives of people.

◆    ◆    ◆

When St. Francis prayed to sow love where there is hatred, he did so knowing love counteracts hatred in the same way light reduces darkness and pardon and forgiveness promote healing and reconciliation.

The wisdom of sowing love lies in understanding hate is a condition one can ill-afford because it spreads toxicity to all areas of life.

Physically, hatred contributes to ulcers, cancer, heart attacks, headaches, skin rashes, and asthma.

Intellectually, it poisons thoughts and diminishes creativity.

Emotionally, it stirs up feelings leading to conflict, strife, and the use of force with the intent to harm.

Relationally, hatred destroys trust needed to establish affirming, supportive, and growth producing relationships.

The poet Goethe demonstrated what is possible when love is sown in the lives of people. "If I treat you as you are," he said, [and you are my enemy because you have injured or offended me in some way] "that is how you will remain. But if I treat you as if you were already the person you could be [and that is my friend] that is the person you will become."

◆    ◆    ◆

While love is the most talked about, the most sung about, and the most written about area of human experience, it is also the most misunderstood because, in large measure, we are not sure what love is.

At the present time love is thought to be feeling and is presented as such in the media.

Several difficulties are associated with love as feeling, the first being it disregards an obvious fact of human experience, namely, that while feelings of love are normally present when one person loves another, each one of us has days when feelings of love for the special person(s) in our life are not present.

It is said feelings are fickle, like a yo yo up one moment and down the next, and like the tide, always coming and going, which suggests that if love is understood as feeling, when days come along in which feelings of love for the special person(s) in our life are not present, it is easy to conclude, "I must no longer love you because I don't feel good about you today."

◆　　　◆　　　◆

It might be well to ask, "How did we come to view love as feeling?

While several factors have contributed to this process, society's acceptance of and adherence to the myth of romantic love ranks among the most influential.

The basic idea of romantic love is that individuals establish relationships based on how they feel which translates, at least theoretically into "The stronger my feelings are for you, the more I love you."

The seductive aspect of romantic love, however, is that it isn't love at all, but rather an attempt on the part of individuals to build relationships for what they can get rather than what they can give and oneness is never achieved.

Relationships established on the basis of feeling are limited in scope and depth because they lack the strength needed to permit individuals to remain their own person, separate and self-determining.

It is at the point of falling out of love, however, that the myth of romantic love works most destructively as few individuals recognize coming apart as an opportunity to build a deep and lasting relationship.

Only when the love that brings people together is commitment do people build the kind of relationships in which the needs and interests of both persons are met, relational aloneness is avoided, and relationships are free from the contaminating effects of distortion.

◆　　　◆　　　◆

Love became a problem of considerable scope in the days following World War II when social forces set in motion by that struggle began rolling wave-after-wave across society, reweaving its fabric, restructuring its institutions, and accelerating the pace, scope, and demands of life to such an extent that people began to feel taxed to the limit to cope. People hard pressed to cope with life lose perspective.

While, in general, results wrought by social forces since World War II have proven beneficial and helpful, some have worked to the detriment of society and its people, in particular the

- radical modification of the system of values, beliefs, traditions, practices, and principles that for so long served as guidelines for behavior and brought unity, continuity, and consistency to the lives of people because, they were shared

- removal of religion as the cement of society

- defining of sex as a need rather than a desire or passion to be fulfilled within the context of human sexuality, and the

- creation of relational vacuums within society making it more difficult for people to establish relationships in which their needs and those of society can be met.

◆          ◆          ◆

Movement of the social forces mentioned led many to feel the nation was forsaking its spiritual heritage and, in fact, had lost its way.

Many felt the removal of religion as the cement of society deprived them of a dimension of life in which they had always found meaning, purpose, and direction; a sense of personal worth and value; and an understanding of what they were to say with their lives.

What had happened was that with religion removed as the cement of society people felt their only option was to look for these in things external to themselves.

What they found was that nothing external, nothing the world values brings meaning, purpose, contentment, and inner peace.

While external factors may help people determine what they want to do with their lives, they are of no value whatsoever when it came to helping them identify what they wanted to say with their lives.

◆          ◆          ◆

The same social forces that removed religion as the cement of society also defined sex as a need, paving the way for unprecedented sexual activity outside of marriage, the rationalizing of sexual intercourse as meeting needs, the equating of sex with love, and the choice of sexual intercourse as the primary means of giving and receiving love.

◆     ◆     ◆

While the social forces that have avalanched upon America over the past half-century have changed society in many ways, one thing they have not done is erase the desire present in all of us to be an integral part of the life of another person.

John Powell, a contemporary writer has wisely observed no one can develop in this world and find a full life apart from relationships that affirm, encourage, and promote growth, an observation validated by the poet Goethe who said, *"If you have one person in your life with whom you can share your innermost being that person will make life a garden for you."*

These things are so because as God saw in the Garden of Eden it is not good for man to be alone where others are concerned.

It is the desire to avoid this kind of aloneness that motivates us to establish relationships in which our needs and those of society can be met, and we can have our uniqueness, specialness, and separateness acknowledged and affirmed by persons emotionally significant to us.

◆     ◆     ◆

Jesus and Paul enjoyed relationships. Jesus' relationship to the twelve men chosen to be His disciples was close, tender, open, and proper. He accepted them when they neither believed He was who He said He was, understood His mission, or grasped His message. Even when one of them betrayed Him and another denied Him, and the others ran away, He refused to break relationship with them.

Relationships meant much to Paul as well. In the salutations to his letters he made it a point to send greeting to individuals he regarded as fellow-laborers.

One of the men considered a fellow-laborer was Philemon, whom, it would appear, was converted under Paul's ministry.

But, Philemon was also a slave owner whose slave, Onesimus, had escaped and fled to Rome where he, too, was converted under Paul's ministry.

Though Onesimus had been quite helpful to him, Paul felt it his duty to send Onesimus back to his master, Philemon.

Drawing upon the strength of his relationship with Philemon, Paul writes a brief, but moving letter in which he says, "Onesimus is more than your slave. He is your Christian brother. Though he ran away, he needs a good relationship with you, his master and Christian brother. It is not good for the two of you to be out of relationship. Forgive him and restore him to favor."

◆     ◆     ◆

These are challenging times for society, its people, and the world, for as the poet Whittier observed over a century ago, *"Hate is strong and mocks the song of peace on earth, goodwill to men."*

Only when the love sown in the lives of people is commitment are men likely to find meaning, purpose, and direction for their lives, and have their needs and those of society met in the relationships they establish.

Only when love in the lives of people is commitment is relational aloneness avoided, and the kinds of experiences men yearn for in relationships with persons emotionally significant to them are possible.

◆     ◆     ◆

Jesus presented love as a commandment, as something men were to do. His words are quite clear. *"You shall love the Lord your God with all your heart and with all your soul and with all your mind, and your neighbor as yourself."* (Matthew 22:37)

As love is not an option and Jesus' command cannot be filled by simply feeling good about someone, consider the following as a model for loving in the way Jesus has commanded.

"Love is the voluntary and deliberate exercise of the human will (my personal capacity to choose) to meet the needs (those things essential to the personhood and well-being of another person) and act in the best interests (those things which build, enhance, support, affirm, and contribute to the well being of others) in spite of what my feelings happen to be."

Love understood as a commitment of one's capacity to choose means love is neither withheld nor withdrawn from others, be they enemies or friends in the absence of feelings of love.

◆     ◆     ◆

John records Jesus demonstrating this kind of love toward an adulterous woman and her accusers in the Temple at Jerusalem (John 8:1-11).

Returning from the Mount of Olives one morning, Jesus enters the Temple and begins teaching the people. John does not disclose where Jesus was in the Temple; however, as it is religious leaders who bring the woman, it can be assumed He was in or near the Court of the Woman (located most likely just inside the main entrance to the Temple).

The drama unfolds in this manner. The Scribes and Pharisees approach bringing a woman whom they say has been taken in the very act of adultery.

Setting her in the midst of those present, they say to Jesus, "Master [KJV] or "Teacher," [NIV], this woman was caught in the act of adultery."

Most likely, the men who translated these versions of Scripture chose to use titles of "Master" and "Teacher" as a means of clarifying the relationship between Jesus and the Scribes and Pharisees.

As a form of address "Master" emphasized the authority Jesus exercised over men who had identified with Him, accepted His authority, and pledged obedience to Him. It was the form of address by which disciples said to Jesus, "We have linked our fate with yours."

It might well be that the scene in Pilate's courtyard played out the way it did because having identified with Jesus, accepted His teachings, and pledged loyalty and obedience to Him, Peter recognized he might be required to share the fate of Jesus; therefore, his attempts to dissociate himself from Jesus, going so far as to deny knowing Him.

And it could be that biblical translators used "Master" and "Teacher" to expose the motives of the Scribes and Pharisees in bringing the woman to Jesus. As they had neither identified with Him, accepted his teachings as authoritative, nor pledged loyalty and obedience to Him, their use of "Master" in addressing Jesus amounted to sarcasm.

Then it isn't clear in what capacity these religious leaders were acting. If acting in a strictly legal capacity their intent being to charge the woman with adultery, the man involved would have been present (adultery being a crime against society and a punishable offense).

In addition, if acting in a legal capacity, an accusation as serious as adultery would more appropriately have been made in the Hall of Hewn Stones where proceedings of the highest court of the land, the Sanhedrin, were held.

And finally, using a cryptic question to elicit what both parties knew the Law said on the subject of adultery is further grounds for questioning the actions of the Scribes and Pharisees in bringing the woman.

"Master," they say, "in the Law Moses commanded us to stone such women. Now what do you say?"

The Scribes and Pharisees were aware that Jesus was versed in the Law; therefore, as aware as they that the penalty for adultery was death by stoning.

Stoning was a form of capital punishment in Israel. Usually stoning took place outside the city walls in the presence of witnesses and members of the community with witnesses against the accused casting the first stones. With regard to the woman in question, as witnesses to her adultery the Scribes and Pharisees would have cast the first stones. Then, as stoning was an offense against the entire community, members of the community also cast stones.

◆     ◆     ◆

All things considered, it seems patently obvious that the motivation for bringing the woman to Jesus had little to do with upholding the Law or purifying the moral climate of society, for had the woman committed adultery (a charge that is neither discussed or disputed), the Scribes and Pharisees had access to the highest court in the land; therefore, no reason at all for bringing her to Jesus.

All things considered, the religious leaders bringing the women to Jesus constituted something of an ad hoc committee formed for the purpose of maneuvering Him into a position in which He could be accused of disregarding the Law or taking some step that would bring Him into conflict with Roman authorities.

If, in response to the alleged charge of adultery Jesus says, "Stone her," He can be charged with inciting others to kill, a charge certain to come to the attention of Roman authorities who had withheld from Jews the right to put a person to death.

If, on the other hand, Jesus does not pronounce the sentence of the Law upon her, He can be accused of condoning adultery (which would discredit Him in the eyes of the people for whom adultery was a crime against society deserving of stoning).

Two options are open to Jesus at this point. He must pass judgment upon the woman and risk conflicting with Roman authority or refuse to pass judgment upon her and appear to disregard the Law.

Jesus does neither.

Instead, He stoops down and begins to write on the ground with His finger, something people did when they wanted to give the impression of being preoccupied or wished to be deliberately inattentive.

In light of the fact that their attempt at discrediting Jesus had failed, coupled with the fact that He said nothing, and by writing on the ground was deliberately inattentive to men used to commanding attention, the situation must have been particularly awkward to the Scribes and Pharisees.

When they continue pressing Him for an answer, Jesus says, *"If any one of you is without sin, let him be the first to throw a stone,"* then * He resumes writing on the ground.

It is interesting to speculate what Jesus wrote. If, as the text says, the woman had been made to stand before the group, it is possible that she was the only one in position to read what He wrote.

In view of her display of courage at a time when her life literally hung in the balance, it may be that Jesus wrote something that gave her courage or spoke to her of love.

◆    ◆    ◆

Taking a step back from the drama played out in the Temple, let's assess the love demonstrated by the several parties involved.

The Accusers. Scribes and Pharisees, religious leaders willing to expose a woman to public humiliation for the purpose of maneuvering an adversary into a position in which they can accuse Him of disregarding the Law or violating some aspect of relationship with Rome.

It would appear that neither the behavior of the woman nor the moral climate of the community (adultery being a serious crime) was of particular concern to the Scribes and Pharisees. Had they been concerned about these things they had access to the highest court in the land and the chances are good that some present were members of the Sanhedrin.

The Accused. Her name is never given. She endures the shame and humiliation of public accusation without uttering a word, attempting to rationalize her behavior, endeavoring to blame others for her actions, or copping out on the environment. If she had, indeed, committed adultery, and from Jesus' comment (8:11) it would appear she had, she knew she had sinned and deserved to be stoned.

The Advocate. In effect, by refusing to pass sentence upon the woman, what Jesus did was elevate the issue of adultery to a higher, more honest level than that at which the Scribes and Pharisees were operating.

At the level of having committed adultery for which stoning was the appropriate punishment, perhaps, no one except the woman was guilty. At the level of being without sin, however, all were guilty.

The end of the matter is this. *"But they having heard Jesus' words, and by their conscience being convicted, went out one by one, beginning from the elder ones until the last."* (KJV)

Left alone with the woman, Jesus says to her, *"Has no one condemned you? Neither do I. Go now and leave your life of sin."*

◆     ◆     ◆

Jesus pointed to love as the characteristic by which the world would distinguish His disciples from other men.

Paul identified love as a more excellent way than faith or hope, a virtue of such quality, depth, and breadth that a special word—agape—was needed to express it.

The significant thing about agape is not that it is an unconditional love, but that it is a love of the will rather than the emotions. It speaks of love that passes human understanding because it is love expressed not so much for what a person is as for who they are.

Paul declared love a more excellent than faith and hope, because

• it is patient, kind, and long suffering, that is, it exercises self-restraint and withholds anger

• it is neither jealous nor boastful. Love does not permit an individual to become so enamored or impressed with his/her importance as to exalt himself/herself above others as to become prideful and conceited as actions of this kind lead inevitably to envy and jealousy.

In addition, love

• is neither arrogant nor rude, for not only is arrogance the antithesis of love, rudeness kills it

• does not insist on its own way. The person possessed by love promotes healing and reconciliation between themselves and their offenders rather than entertain thoughts of retaliation or getting even

• is neither irritable or resentful or touchy. Having removed the offenses of others to a place in their lives as far from offence as the East is from the West in the universe, followers of Christ forego holding grudges as that would necessitate calling to mind offences that have been forgiven

• does not rejoice in wrong; instead it rejoices in right and truth. It rejoices in all things that can be believed, hoped for, or endured with a good conscience

• bears all things, believes all things, and endures all things, that is, it holds up against privations and hardships without questioning the integrity of others, and it continues to believe even when others have ceased to do so.

It has been said that men are turned off by disappointment, turned inward by discouragement, turned out by their behavior, but turned on by love. "Where there is hatred let me sow love."

# 3

# *WHERE THERE IS INJURY LET ME SOW PARDON*

o o o o o o o o o o o o o o o o o o o o o o o o o o o o o o
*"Pardon and forgiveness like a poultice heal the injured and reconcile them to those who have injured them."*

—*Paraphrase*

Having prayed God make him an instrument of peace that he might sow love where there is hatred, St. Francis continued his prayer requesting that he sow pardon where there was injury.

While this saintly man did not clarify what he meant by injury, it seems reasonable to suppose that for him injury was any thought, feeling, or behavior that wounds men in the core of their being prompting them to react in ways that lead to conflict, strife, violence, and the use of force with the intent to do harm.

◆　　　◆　　　◆

Scripture presents injury as offenses (sins, debts, trespasses, and transgressions) of such seriousness that they can neither be condoned, excused, denied, minimized, nor absolved by a socially acceptable, "I'm sorry."

For instance, the word translated "debts" or "trespasses" in the Lord's Prayer is derived from a noun meaning "to owe." Matthew uses this word when speaking of offenses serious enough as to require reparation on the part of an offender (Matthew 6:12), while Paul uses it to specify debts for which payment is due (Romans (15:27).

What it is that motivates men to injure one another?

Where does violence originate? Could it be that humankind is inherently violent? Is violence in our genes?

Approximately twenty years ago, in their report to the American Academy of Child Psychiatry, a panel of child psychiatrists voiced concern that children were growing up in a society in which violence was accepted as a way of life.

As America moves into a Twenty-First Century, violence is all-encompassing and so lacking in motive and reason that one is persuaded the foreign observer was right who remarked that murder was as much a part of the American way of life as hot dogs and Coca-Cola, and that former Attorney General Janet Reno might have been right when she suggested that perhaps America had become numb to violence because it is, in fact, drowning in it.

◆　　　◆　　　◆

Delegates to the Constitution Convention wove violence into the fabric of our national life by writing into the Constitution doctrines that contradicted truths Jefferson said were self-evident, namely, that all men were created equal, endowed by their Creator with certain rights that were unalienable, among them life, liberty, and the pursuit of happiness.

Regrettably, our founding fathers also wrote into the Constitution provisions that relegated slaves and Indians to second-class citizenship, thereby, severely limiting their participation in the life of the nation for nearly a hundred years.

Even after the Thirteenth Amendment sounded the death knell of slavery, another hundred years would pass before the last vestiges of second-class citizenship would be removed by law.

◆　　　◆　　　◆

In view of these observations, it seems apparent that violence reflects the value system selected by men and nations as guidelines for their lives.

When the spiritual and social consciousness of a country is radically altered as was that of the United States following World War II, and values that had for so long served as guidelines for society and its people, bound them together and brought continuity and consistency to their lives are lost, rejected, or replaced, conditions favorable to conflict are created, and in time violence becomes a way of life and an accepted response to injury.

Today, violence is so pervasive that it is no longer recognized as the personal, social, economic, political, and spiritual problem it is.

Not only that, but violence is so profitable that media executives continue to ignore findings linking violence with aggression because it sells movies, videos, and television time. In addition, violence is so ingrained in the public mind that many refuse to acknowledge the existence of any relationship between guns and violence.

On one of her compact discs, entertainer Ann Murray sings a song titled, *A Little Good News,* the lyrics of which tell of a local paper containing one more sad story than the reader can stand, and a longing for headlines that say, *"Not much to print today, can't find much bad to say."*

What the reader of that newspaper desired were headlines declaring, *"nobody robbed a liquor store on the lower part of town. Nobody OD'd, nobody burned a single building down. Nobody fired a shot in anger, nobody had to die in vain."* That would be good news any day.[1]

◆     ◆     ◆

Pardon and forgiveness are theologically sound, psychologically healthy, and relationally beneficial remedies for injury.

They are sound theologically because they are what God does when we injure Him.

They are healthy psychologically because it is better to pardon and forgive those who injure us rather than live with toxic thoughts, feelings, and behaviors generated by injury.

And they are beneficial relationally because they encourage the injured to rise above what has happened to them and forego thoughts of retaliation and getting even rather than risk damaging relationships beyond their capacity to meet the needs of people and ward off the kind of aloneness God saw was not good for men.

As it is how individuals feel about what happens to them that paves the way to violence and the use of force with the intent to harm, it is clearly in the best interest of society and its people to incorporate pardon and forgiveness into their system of values as the healthiest and most appropriate responses one can make to injury.

---

1.   *A Little Good News* was included on a compact disc titled, *The Very Best of Anne Murray,* distributed by Cema Special Markets.

◆    ◆    ◆

To encourage healing and reconciliation those who have been injured must remove the transgressions of their offenders to a place as far from offense in their lives as the East is from the West in the universe, and remember them against their offenders no more.

Removing the sins and trespasses of offenders enables those who have been injured to rise above feelings of anger and hostility that so often stand in the way of healing and reconciliation.

◆    ◆    ◆

By definition, pardon and forgiveness are responses intentionally chosen or courses of action set in motion in the wake of injury.

Forgiveness is a decision to make peace with the past, to look beyond what has happened in the interest of healing and reconciliation.

And, however unfair it may seem, the burden of pardon and forgiveness always falls upon the injured.

Beverly Flannigan spoke with great wisdom when she declared only the brave pardon and forgive those who trespass against them.[2]

To forgive the injured must be brave enough to confront their pain, courageous enough to chose forgiveness over resentment and hatred, and gallant enough to remove sins and trespasses committed against them to a place in their lives as far from retaliation and getting even as the East is from the West in the universe.

With offenses committed against them removed and their offenders pardoned the injured are free to focus on healing, reconciliation, and a happier, more productive life.

◆    ◆    ◆

It is essential to understand that in the same way God for His own sake pardons and forgives those who sin and trespass against Him (Isaiah 43:25), that

---

2.    Beverly Flanigan, "Unforgivable War Crimes Of The Heart," *Psychology Today* (September-October, 1992), p. 39.

pardoning and forgiving those who sin and trespass against us is something we do for ourselves.

Rather than withhold remedies that heal and promote reconciliation and reap the destructive harvest injury inflicts upon one's body, mind, and soul, it seems wise to forgive rather than run the risk that strife, conflict, and violence with the intent to harm will follow.

◆     ◆     ◆

Choosing to pardon and forgive one's offenders is a sign of spiritual obedience, psychological health, and relational wisdom. It signifies that in their own eyes the injured see themselves as too noble to permit injury to dictate the course of life.

In addition, pardoning and forgiving one's offenders is relationally beneficial as it lessens the possibility that relationships will be fractured beyond their capacity to meet the needs of people and help them avoid relational aloneness.

As nothing is gained by permitting a situation that has the potential of resulting in broken relationships and relational aloneness to continue until it erupts in conflict, violence, and possible harm, it seems wise to pardon and forgive those who injure us.

◆     ◆     ◆

To promote healing and reconciliation, instruments of peace must demonstrate the value of pardon and forgiveness as remedies for injury and acquaint those who have been injured with what is required to apply them.

When intentionally chosen, remedies of pardon and forgiveness enable the injured to detach from their injury, remove the sins of offenders, and refuse to call to mind offenses which their offenders have reason to believe have been forgiven.

Some aspects relating to pardon and forgiveness are easily misunderstood. Among these is the idea that forgiveness overlooks what has happened and lets people off the hook.

Forgiveness neither overlooks what has happened, nor does it let people off the hook. Forgiveness is simply letting go of or looking beyond what has happened, freeing the injured and those who have injured them to move in the direction of healing and reconciliation.

Neither does forgiveness require offences be forgotten as forgetting nullifies the value of experience and negates opportunities for learning from one's experience.

Rather than forget the sins and trespasses of those who offend us, the wisest, healthiest, and most beneficial thing one can do is follow God's example; pardon and forgive one's offenders, remove their offenses, and remember them against these people no more.

◆          ◆          ◆

Having demonstrated the value of pardon and forgiveness, instruments of peace can help those who are injured to accept, control, and express the anger injury generates.

The Apostle Paul said, *"Be angry but sin not."* What he is saying to those who are injured is, "Its okay to be angry when injured, but don't allow anger to cause you to sin."

To control and express anger without allowing that emotion to move them in the direction of conflict, violence, and the use of force with intent to harm, the injured must acquire the self-mastery and self-control needed to vent their feelings in ways not likely to prove destructive to themselves or their relationships.

To acquire these virtues the injured must decide what is important and unimportant and learn to perceive things correctly.

Deciding what is important and unimportant lessens the possibility of becoming angry over things that don't really matter while perceiving things correctly helps prevent the expression of anger when anger isn't called for.

It has been said that while what happens to us is important, it is more important how we feel about what has happened.

Therefore, when what happens to us is deemed to be more important than how we feel about what has happened, we are likely to retaliate or attempt to get even with those who have injured them.

If, however, how we feel is deemed more important than what has happened, we are likely to choose pardon and forgiveness as a response.

◆          ◆          ◆

On balance, America is a good and decent nation whose people have always found the courage to act decisively when faced with a clear and present danger.

Beyond the efforts of individuals, it may be time for society and its people to

• recognize violence as a personal, social, economic, political, and spiritual problem, and commit ourselves to pardon and forgiveness as remedies to injury in preference to retaliation and getting even

• remind our public officials that what happens on the streets of our cities is more important than what happens on Mars

• adopt measures that have proven effective deterrents of violence—especially the certainty of punishment via more police, quicker trials, and higher conviction rates

• recognize that where movie moguls, television executives, and book publishers are concerned the bottom line is, projects that do not make money are soon cancelled

• acknowledge that while it is our constitutional right to own a gun, that it may be time to voluntarily limit this right

• accept that while everyone struggles with their neighbors, violence that knows no bounds and has no motive will no longer be condoned and allowed to continue as an acceptable way of settling differences?

And finally, in the interest of promoting healing and reconciliation in situations where hatred might prompt men to react in ways that lead to conflict strife, violence, and the use of force with the intent to do harm, it may be time to rethink our individual and national systems of values, replacing external values with values of the inner life.

◆      ◆      ◆

To acquire traits and characteristics helpful in bringing healing and reconciliation those who are injured must

• detach from their offences and apply remedies of pardon and forgiveness

• keep in mind that while injury throws all areas of life out of balance pardon and forgiveness restores balance to life

• acquire the strength of character necessary to remain focused on healing and reconciliation

• desire to be filled with the good things of God that come to those who forgive their offenders, pardon offences committed against them, and refuse to bring them up again

• show compassion to the injured and themselves as well as both need healing

• accept the reality that in a society in which retaliation and getting even are accepted as responses to injury that to advocate pardon and forgiveness is to be viewed as wimps and weaklings by those opposed to Christ.

◆          ◆          ◆

Jesus spoke to those who would be instruments of His peace when He said, *"If you* [pardon and] *forgive men their trespasses [their reckless and willful sins leaving them, letting them go, and giving up resentment when they sin and transgress against you in ways that injure] your heavenly Father will also forgive you. But if you do not forgive men their sins* [when they injure you], *your Father will not* [pardon and] *forgive your sins."* (Annotated paraphrase)

# 4

# *WHERE THERE IS DOUBT LET ME SOW FAITH*

o o o o o o o o o o o o o o o o o o o o o o o o o o o o o o o

*"Doubt is a pain too lonely to know that faith is his twin brother."*

—*Kahlil Gibran*

Having prayed the Lord make him an instrument of peace, sowing love where there was hatred and pardon where there was injury, St. Francis continued, *"Where there is doubt let me sow faith."*

Faith is the clearest evidence of God in the lives of men, and together with virtues of hope and love, the cornerstone of religious living.

What has always been a matter of debate, however, is the relationship of faith and doubt, the question being is there room for doubt in matters of faith?

Does doubt imply diminished faith or suggest an absence of faith?

If faith is understood as believing something is true, then in the same way hatred is diminished love, doubt could be said to be diminished or qualified faith, with strong doubt constituting unbelief.

To theologian Paul Tillich faith is a state of being ultimately concerned. While men have concerns other than the spiritual, some painfully urgent, when ultimately concerned all concerns are subordinated to that of the spiritual or rejected them altogether.[1]

♦     ♦     ♦

---

1.   Paul Tillich, *Dynamics of Faith* (New York: Harper & Brothers, 1957), p. 1.

On a continuum the meaning of doubt ranges from simple questioning to being uncertain, astonished, and perplexed; divided in mind and judgment, of two opinions; hesitant, at a loss as to how to proceed, determine, speak, and act to a direct antithesis of faith.

The Gospels contain four accounts in the ministry of Jesus in which doubt plays a major role.

### Doubt in the Life of Peter
### Matthew 15:29-35

In Mark 7:31, Jesus and the disciples are in the vicinity of Tyre on the shore of the Mediterranean Sea.

Accompanied by a crowd of several thousands, they depart traveling in a southeasterly direction through Sidon and the region of Decapolis, arriving late afternoon three days and seventy miles later in the vicinity of the Sea of Galilee.

Having been on the road for several days at a time when people seldom traveled far enough from home as to require an overnight stay the people are weary and their food supply is exhausted.

Being in a desolate place with the Sabbath approaching, the disciples request Jesus send the people away that they might exercise the right of travelers and find food and lodging in the surrounding villages and countryside.

*"In such a remote place, how can we feed so many people with what we have,"* they ask. *"Where can we get enough bread to feed them?"*

Sensing the people weak from lack of food and fearing they might faint if sent away without being feed, Jesus says, *"I have pity and sympathy and am deeply moved for the crowd, because they have been with Me now three days and they have nothing [at all left] to eat...."* (Annotated)

At the moment according to Matthew, Luke, and John, the disciples have five loaves and two fish (Mark says the number of fish was seven), which, according to John belong to a boy in the crowd.

Whether furnished by the disciples, the boy, or both, Jesus takes the loaves and the fish, instructs the people to sit down and says a blessing, perhaps, the blessing said before a Jewish meal, *"Blessed art thou, O Lord our God, king of the world, who hast brought forth bread from the earth."* Then he creates food and the people are fed.

Meanwhile news comes of the beheading of John the Baptist, prompting Jesus to send the crowd on their way (most likely taking with them some of the broken pieces of bread and fish gathered up after the feeding) and then to dismiss the disciples with instructions to go ahead of Him by boat to the city of Bethsaida while He remains behind to pray.

◆      ◆      ◆

The Sea of Galilee is thirteen miles long and eight miles wide, surrounded on three sides by cliffs that rise to a height of twelve to fifteen hundred feet.

At night when temperatures drop, cool winds rushing down the slopes from the East strike the warm surface of the Lake stirring up sudden and violent storms.

On the evening in question, the disciples are in the middle of the lake when a storm strikes. As they are yet several miles from their destination rowing into the teeth of the storm they strain at their oars to make progress.

Sometime during the fourth watch, that is, between three and six a.m., His time of prayer ended, Jesus comes to them walking on the water.

Thinking Him a ghost or spirit, the disciples are terrified. Upon being assured that it is Jesus, Peter, the impulsive disciple, asks that he be commanded to come to Jesus on the water.

When Jesus bids him *"Come,"* Peter courageously steps out of the boat and begins walking to Jesus. Soon, however, he becomes fearful and begins to sink at which point he cries, *"Lord, save me."*

Reaching out to Peter, Jesus takes him by the hand, and together they climb into the boat.

Safely in the boat Jesus says to Peter, *"You of little faith, why did you doubt?"* (Mt. 14:22-31 Annotated).

Jesus' words to Peter translate a word that could reasonably be paraphrased as "half-believer" or "doubter."

◆      ◆      ◆

## Jesus Addresses the Eroding Effect of Doubt
### Matthew 21:18-21

Following the incident biblical interpreters call the cleansing of the Temple, Jesus leaves Jerusalem and journeys the short distance to Bethany where He finds lodging for the night, most likely with His friends Mary, Martha, and Lazarus.

Returning to the city the next morning, Jesus sees a fig tree with leaves but no fruit on it. *"Let no fruit grow on thee henceforward for ever more,"* He says, and the tree withers immediately. (KJV)

In the ancient world it was believed that a curse or woe pronounced by a righteous man contained the power to bring it to pass.

When the disciples marvel at how quickly the fig tree has withered, Jesus takes the opportunity to comment on the eroding effect of doubt.

He suggests faith the size of a mustard seed would enable men to wither a fig tree as He had done, or say to a mountain, "Move from here to there" and it would move.

Faith the size of a mustard seed would have enabled Peter to continue on the water to Jesus.

But the faith to walk on water, shrivel fig trees, move mountains, or receive things of God must be without doubt. There can be no question that such things are possible to men of faith.

### Jesus Predicts His Betrayal
### John 13:18-22

The scene is Jerusalem. It is spring, the time of Passover, the first of three great feasts celebrating events in the life of the Hebrews people.

Knowing He is soon to leave Jesus has arranged to eat a last Passover meal with the disciples. Before eating the Supper, Jesus discards His outer garment, girds Himself with a towel and proceeds to wash the feet of the disciples.

When He has finished and has returned to His place at the table Jesus interprets the meaning of what He has done before informing the disciples that one of their number is going to betray Him (John 13:22).

The disciples are stunned and perplexed. At a loss to believe that such a thing could be true, that one of them would betray Him, and uncertain as to what they are to say or do, the disciples simply stare at each other.

It remains for Jesus to resolve the situation by dipping a morsel of bread in the wine and giving it to Judas.

### Jesus Addresses Doubt Relating to Whether
### He is the Christ
### John 10:22-24

Jesus also spoke of doubt to some of the religious leaders of Israel.

In all likelihood Jesus and the disciples began their journey to Jerusalem in late November as John records Jesus walking on Solomon's Porch (located on the east side of the outer Court of the Gentiles) during the Feast of Dedication (Hanukkah) celebrated in early December to commemorate the dedication of the altar in the Temple at Jerusalem in the time of Judas Maccabees (about 170 B.C.).

Among those present with Him are a number of religious leaders who want to know is whether Jesus is the Christ. *"How long are you going to keep us in doubt and suspense?"* they ask. *"If you are really the Christ [the Messiah], tell us so plainly and openly." (Annotated)*

This is the only instance in which Jesus is asked directly, "Are you the Christ?"

If as Peter had declared at Cesarea Philipi, *"You are the Christ,"* then Jesus is Messiah and He stands at the center of the religious establishment of Israel, the One for whom the people had been looking.

While Jesus had revealed who He was and something of His mission to a Samaritan woman at Jacob's well and a blind man in the Temple, and performed miraculous things which the people believed only God or One sent by God could do, He had not declared publicly that He was Messiah.

Belief in the lives of the religious leaders would have enabled them to recognize Jesus as the Christ. As they have not believed, doubt prompts them to accuse Him of blasphemy and they take up stones to stone Him as someone claiming to be God.

◆          ◆          ◆

St. Francis prayed God would make him an instrument of peace sowing faith where there was doubt.

If as Carl Jung suggests, everyone needs to believe in something or someone above, faith is a simple matter of believing.

Yet, like hate and love, the concept of faith is somewhat ethereal and difficult for many to grasp. To Paul Tillich, faith as understood by a majority of people was so muddled as to be more productive of disease than health, a word subject to more distortion, misunderstanding, and questionable definition than any word in the religious language.[2]

The writer of the Book of Hebrews goes beyond faith as simply believing and faith as a human need by defining faith as the *"substance of things hoped for, evidence of things not seen."* (KJV)

---

2.     Tillich, ibid, p. ix.

If the word "God" is substituted for "substance" and "evidence" then the substance of what men hope for and the evidence of what man cannot see in their lives, is God.

God is spiritual in His nature. Created in His image men are spiritual beings endowed with faculties that make it possible to know and communicate with Him and resonate to His truth; therefore, faith is largely a subjective or personal matter.

The only way faith can be demonstrated objectively is by recognizing that forces opposed to Christ are going to revile, snub, harass, reject, putdown, discriminate against, and say all manner of evil against followers of Christ whose lives approximate the life of Christ closely.

◆　　　◆　　　◆

In view of these things, how are instruments of peace to sow the antidote of faith where doubt is present? What can be done to help those for whom doubt is a problem in matters of faith?

To begin, as all men have the same range of human experiences, instruments of peace can help followers of Christ accept doubt as part of the religious experience.

In the same way Abraham, revered as a man of faith doubted when promised a child (Genesis 17:17), Moses doubted when told the Lord would give the Hebrews a month's ration of meat in response to their complaining of hardship (Numbers 11:21), Zacharias found it difficult to believe when told he would have a son, and the disciples were unable to heal a demoniac because of doubt (Matthew 17:19), the most dedicated among us is likely to doubt one time or another as everyone experiences dark nights of the soul in which God seems far from us and our prayers seem to rise no farther than the ceiling.

Most of us tend to doubt when we fail to achieve a goal we set for ourselves and ties with persons emotionally significant to us are severed in experiences of loss. We tend to doubt when help for which we have prayed is not forthcoming.

◆　　　◆　　　◆

In addition to helping people accept doubt as an element of faith instruments of peace can sow faith by sharing their "presence" with those in whose lives doubt is present.

Presence is an essential attribute of our humanness and a visible manifestation of the human spirit. It is that quality of our humanness that draws people to another as a magnet draws objects to itself.

Inherent in presence is power to comfort, reassure, and validate the worth and value of individuals in the throes of doubt.

In the same way Jesus' presence was comforting to the disciples on the Sea of Galilee and the presence of the shepherd reassuring to the sheep in Psalm Twenty-Three, the presence of instruments of peace is comforting and reassuring to individuals struggling with doubt in matters of faith as presence helps transform doubt from unbelief into a challenge to grow in faith.

◆     ◆     ◆

Earlier it was noted that the relationship of faith and doubt has always been a matter of debate, the question being does doubt imply diminished faith or the absence of faith?

While for theologian Paul Tillich faith was a legitimate element of faith, for others doubt implies diminished faith, unbelief, or signifies the absence of faith altogether.

Doubt as a legitimate element of faith is manifested three times in the experience of the Apostle Peter.

At Caesarea Philippi, on the basis of faith Peter correctly identified Jesus as the Christ and was commended for that disclosure. *"Blessed are you, Simon son of Jonah, for this was not revealed to you by men, but by my Father in heaven."*

Certainly it was faith that enabled Peter to step out of the boat on the Sea of Galilee with the thought in mind of walking to Jesus, but doubt that caused him to sink.

Yet, in these experiences and later in the courtyard of Pontius Pilate, Peter was confronted by doubt as an element of his faith.

At the Last Supper in Jerusalem, having washed the feet of the disciples and announced that one of them would betray Him, Jesus turns to Peter and says, *"Satan has asked to sift you as wheat. But I have prayed especially for you [Peter] that your own faith may not fail."* (NIV)

From Jesus' statement it would appear He considered doubt a legitimate element of faith, for the word He uses in speaking to Peter does not imply a total extinction or lack of faith.

Therefore, continues Jesus, *"When you have turned again,"* [from your experience of having denied me as a penitent returns after sinning], *"strengthen and establish your brethren."* (Annotated)

♦     ♦     ♦

To understand the working of doubt in the lives of men as demonstrated in the life of Peter, we need to review what it meant to be a disciple in the time of Jesus.

To be a disciple meant more than simply being a pupil or learner. It involved identifying with a teacher, pledging one's loyalty to that person, and accepting his teaching as the rule for one's life.

In effect, becoming a disciple meant identifying with a teacher so closely that one's fate was linked to the fate of that person.

In light of these comments, Peter's denial of Jesus can be understood, in part, as the moment in which Peter was forced to come to grips with what discipleship might cost him.

Therefore, might not the intensity with which Peter attempts to dissociate himself from Jesus, going so far as to deny knowing Him, can be attributed to the fact that he feared he might be required to share Jesus' fate?

*"This man was with him,"* says a passing servant girl to which Peter responds, *"I don't know him."*

Later someone says to Peter, *"You also are one of them,"* suggesting Peter was recognized as one of the band of disciples. To this person Peter responds, *"Man, I am not!"*

About an hour later a third person asserts Peter was with Jesus. This time Peter responds, *"Man, I don't know what you are speaking about!"*

Even as Peter speaks, the rooster crows a third time, Jesus turns and looks in Peter's direction, and Peter remembers the words Jesus had spoken to him, *"Before the rooster crows today, you will disown me three times."*

Doubt having eroded the strength of his faith, Scripture says Peter went outside and wept bitterly.

# 5

# *WHERE THERE IS DESPAIR LET ME SOW HOPE*

o o o o o o o o o o o o o o o o o o o o o o o o o o o o o o o o o o

*"We did not dare to breathe a prayer or give our anguish scope. Something was dead in each in each of us. And what was dead was hope."*

—Oscar Wilde, *Ballad of Reading Gaol*

Having prayed the Lord make him an instrument of peace, sowing love where there was hatred, pardon where there was injury, and faith where there was doubt St. Francis continued, *"Where there is despair, let me sow hope."*

Hope is the act of anticipating a future. It was the hope of ancient Israel, for instance, that a time would come when the lion would lie down with the lamb, all nature would be at peace, men would beat their spears into plowshares, and learn war no more.

Writing to Christians at Corinth, Paul identified hope, faith, and love as virtues that endure.

Yet, while hope is inseparable from faith and love, we hear less of it, most likely because hope is the most subjective of the three virtues, hard to define, and even harder to conceptualize and live out.

It may be that we hear less of hope because in an age obsessed with an aggressive, results-oriented, achievement-minded approach to life, hope doesn't come off as a power word. It's much too tame to mobilize people to give "a hundred and ten percent."

♦　　♦　　♦

How curious it is, therefore, that while everyone is not a person of faith, and if Joan Callwood is correct, not everyone can love, that the testimony of history and experience should be that both men and nations live their lives in hope.

In the same way Faith is the upward glance of the soul drawing humankind to God, Hope is the forward glance of the soul that enables men and women to endure present difficulties and keep on keeping on when everything has been taken from them.

Writing to his friend, Eberhard Bethge, Detrieth Bonhoffer said, "*If we survive all this [meaning the war] we shall be able to see quite clearly that all has all turned out for the best. Therefore, we have every reason to hope.*"

As long as men have hope they are not controlled by events past or present. While they may know defeat, experience starvation, lose their possessions, be denied their liberty, deprived of their freedom, and face the possibility that life itself will be taken from them, as long as they have hope they are not likely to despair.

♦　　♦　　♦

This thought was impressed upon me at an untimely hour with incredible force several years ago when I was awakened at three a.m. and informed that my oldest living friend had just taken his life in what authorities described as the most perfectly executed act of self destruction they had ever witnessed.

While growing up we enjoyed many good times on the farm where he lived.

We laughed when he milked the cows and all the cats assembled for what they considered their share of fresh milk.

We ran races that I always won, not because I was necessarily a faster runner, but because he couldn't run without laughing and I couldn't laugh and run.

In adult life, my friend became my brother-in-law. One day, while fighting a fire he lost a large percentage of his hearing when some chemicals exploded, and for the remainder of his life wore a hearing aid in each ear.

Tragic indeed! But the tragic aspect of that day was not that my friend lost his hearing, but that the loss of hearing disqualified him from being an active fire-fighter, a profession that brought meaning and purpose to his life.

Though assured a job and college education for his children he was never able to find a "why" for his life. In time, he withdrew from involvement in his community, his marriage fell victim to the depression that overwhelmed him, and he despaired of life itself.

Apparently, those around him were unaware of and alert to signs present when hope goes out of a human life. For that reason, no one pointed him toward those who might have helped.

Life is painfully simple. As long as men have hope they do not despair, but when hope goes out of a man's life, life goes out of that man.

◆    ◆    ◆

Of all the human conditions in which instruments of peace are called to be involved, despair is, perhaps, the most difficult, as despair is anguish of the soul, a deep and abiding feeling that one is without hope.

Despair is the state of being at which individuals arrive having searched a lifetime for meaning in work, pleasure, fame, acquisition, and wealth only to conclude life is vanity, meaningless, an exercise in futility, empty of significance, devoid of hope.

Despair is what Judas was feeling when alienated from the company of the Apostles his attempt at voiding his act of betrayal is nullified by the refusal of the authorities to accept money they had given him. In despair Judas took his life.

◆    ◆    ◆

St. Francis was convinced that in the same way love is the antidote of hate, and pardon and forgiveness bring healing and reconciliation to both the injured and those who injure them, that hope was the remedy for despair.

It was in this vein that Paul said to the Corinthians, "*We are hedged in (pressed) on every side*," [troubled and oppressed in every way] but not cramped or crushed; we suffer embarrassments and are perplexed and unable to find a way out, but not driven to despair." (Annotated)

◆    ◆    ◆

The situation facing all who aspire to be instruments of peace is one of recognizing that men avoid despair only by affirming life is good, that life is intended to be filled with meaning and purpose, abundance and fulfillment, contentment and wholeness, therefore, worth living.

Believing hope to be the antidote to despair, what can instruments of peace do to sow hope where despair is found?

As a first step, instruments of peace can

• acknowledge hope as the faith required to see the light at the end of the tunnel and the motivation to move toward that light

• accept others as they are, where they are, aware men lose hope when cut off from, out of fellowship and communication with, unrelated to, and perhaps, unloved by those around them

• identify factors in society, human experience, and themselves that contribute to despair and set about changing or altering them

• sow the antidote of hope confident it changes the perspective of men and women

• appreciate hope as a gift to be given away no strings attached

• refuse to introduce or condone any form of distortion in relationships as distortion makes for the kind of aloneness God saw was not good

• declare with their lives that there is every reason to hope because it is God that infuses life with meaning, purpose, wholeness, contentment, fulfillment, and abundance

• affirm hope as a reality rather than a "pie in the sky" response given by Christians because they lack a better response to the situations, circumstances, and difficulties confronting individuals around them.

◆　　　◆　　　◆

Regrettably, in view of recent world and national events, many have been led to question whether oil in the lamp of hope is running low. The times are uncertain, the world troubled, and war, continuing acts of terrorism, and an unending cycle of inhumanity dominate the news any day of the week.

Yet, even when the times are out of joint there is reason to declare, *"We have every reason to hope,"* because hope is not eradicated by events or by the most scandalous actions of men

Our ancestors brought to this land the conviction that life has meaning and they enshrined that hope in the Preamble to the Constitution which reads, *"We the People of the United States, in Order to form a more perfect Union, establish Jus-*

*tice, insure domestic Tranquility, provide for the common defense, promote the general Welfare, and secure the blessing of liberty to themselves and our Posterity, do ordain and establish this Constitution for the United States of America."*

It has been said that eternal vigilance is the price of freedom. This being the case, if hope is to endure as an effective antidote of despair, it must again take its place alongside virtues of faith and love in the system of values that govern the lives of men and nations.

Should hope not find its way into these value systems then we stand in peril that confidence in things that stave off despair: meaning, purpose, abundance, and fulfillment, trust in each other, confidence in the integrity of work, and faith in God Himself may be diluted or destroyed.

If these things are permitted to happen, surely we will have gained the whole world but lost what is needed most, hope.

And, parenthetically, lost ourselves as well.

◆     ◆     ◆

What a courageous and constructive act it would be in times as troubled and confused as the present, if each one of us would establish hope in the system of values that guide our lives.

What we must not permit to happen is for hope to be

• buried under an avalanche of "wants" when all we have a right to ask for and all God has promised is that He will meet our needs

• ground under by the machinery necessary to send man to the moon and beyond while the institutions of education and human care struggle with inadequate funds to cope with the pressures of life in a post-modern society, or

• swallowed up by a way of life that ignores the implications of men scrambling madly over the backs of their fellow men, or absorbed by a national conscience so dulled by prosperity and success that the loneliness, heartache, and emptiness of the "have nots" is seldom an object of concern in the minds of the those who have.

◆     ◆     ◆

In the Old Testament the term for hope occurring most often is very close in meaning to the Hebrew word for belief, implying implies rest, leaning on, trust, and confidence in God.[1]

It is hope that enables men

- to walk through life's Valleys of Dark Shadows confident that all is going to turn out for the best

- to accept days in the Valley as times of testing and refining of character.

It is hope

- that encourages us to rest in the Lord and affirm a future though its shape be indefinite,

- from which we derive the faith to affirm all things work for good because we understand "good" as what is good to God.

◆     ◆     ◆

Dietrich Bonhoeffer personified hope as clearly as anyone in the Twentieth Century.

In the years preceding World War II, Bonhoeffer lived and lectured at Union Seminary in New York. As clouds of war gathered over Europe in the late 1930's and events began conspiring to bring about a struggle of global proportions, Bonhoeffer made the fateful decision to return to his homeland.

Once back in Germany, Bonhoeffer discovered he could not, nor would not remain silent where Adolph Hitler and Nazism were concerned.

In time, his opposition to the Third Reich earned him a cell in the infamous Buchenwald Concentration Camp where he remained for two years. As the war progressed armies of the Allied nations began the liberation of Europe. As they drew near Buchenwald, the Gestapo hung Bonhoeffer.

Hanging Bonhoeffer was a futile gesture proving once again that one does not silence the message by killing the messenger, as Bonhoeffer left a priceless heritage

---

1.    James Hastings (editor), *Hastings Dictionary Of The Bible* (Hendrickson Publishers, 1994), p. 361.

in the form of a collection of letters written from prison to parents and friends, letters that bear the stamp of his confidence in God and the role hope played in his life.

This confidence is best expressed in a letter written to his friend, Eberhard Bethge, serving in the German Air Force.

*"Whatever weakness, self reproach, and guilt we attribute to these events [the war] in the events themselves is God. If we survive all this [meaning the war] we shall be able to see quite clearly that all has all turned out for the best."*[2]

◆     ◆     ◆

What was it that led the Apostle Paul to write words of hope to the Church at Corinth and Detriech Bonhoeffer to write words of a similar nature to his friend, Gerhard Bethge?

Each man knew it is hope that gives men confidence to face an uncertain future and affirm that regardless of what the shape of that future might prove to be, that it is in the hand of God.

Christ was the basis of their hope even as he is the author, source, and object of hope in our time. Therefore, while it would appear we have every reason to despair, actually, we have every reason to hope.

"We have very reason to hope." Word written from prison by men facing death, confident things were going to turn out for the best.

---

2.    Dietrich Bonhoeffer, *Letters and Papers from Prison*, ed. Eberhard Bethge, (New York: Simon and Shuster, 1997), p. 191.

# 6

## *WHERE THERE IS DARKNESS LET ME SOW LIGHT*

*"The people who walk in darkness have seen a great light: they that dwell in the land of the shadow of death, upon them hath the light shined."*

—*(KJV)*

Darkness and light appear initially as conditions associated with God's act of creation, darkness being the primordial condition covering the surface of a formless and empty earth, and light the primal luminescence created to separate night from day.

Used in a figurative or non-literal sense in Scripture darkness stands for moral and spiritual ignorance, destruction, ruin, unhappiness, the underworld, and death; light for God's presence, His redemptive activity, truth, holiness, purity, and glory.

To understand the desire of St. Francis' to sow light where darkness exists, it is important to approach light and darkness as conditions of life and survey the way they work in the lives of men.

◆     ◆     ◆

## An Example of Darkness

The Fifth Chapter of John finds Jesus in Jerusalem for one of the annual feasts of Judaism, most likely the Feast of Pentecost celebrating the closing of the harvest.

John sets the scene in these words, *"Now there was in Jerusalem near the Sheep Gate. This pool in the Hebrew is called Bethesda* [which means 'House of Mercy'], having *five* porches (alcoves, colonnades, doorways)."* (John 5:2 Annotated)

Recent excavations below the ruins of the Basilica of St. Anne to the north of the Temple Mount have unearthed a large trapezium shaped double pool divided in the middle by a broad wall corresponding to the description of the pool John mentions.

Each day impotent, paralyzed, blind, lame, and crippled men came to the pool, as it was believed the water had healing properties when stirred by an angel.

While there was no way of anticipating when the waters would be stirred, the stirring must have occurred frequently enough to encourage those in need to spend as much time as possible beside the pool and to return day after day.

To be healed, however, one had to be first into the pool when the waters were disturbed.

◆     ◆     ◆

Among those who came to the pool each day was a man who had been unable to walk for thirty-eight years.

John does not divulge how the man came to be in this condition. The only clue given is contained in Jesus' remark once the man has been healed, *"Go and sin no more, lest a worse thing* (worst than being unable to walk), *come upon thee."*

Each day the lame man was brought to the pool on a light, flexible, but sturdy mat, strong enough to support his weight, but light enough that he is able to pick it up when healed.

Perceiving the need of the man Jesus asks, *"Do you want to be healed?"*

◆     ◆     ◆

It seems reasonable to assume anyone unable to move about under their own power for almost four decades, who had to rely upon others to bring him to the pool each morning and take him home each evening would have responded to Jesus' question with a resounding "Yes."

But the man does not. Instead, he begins a lengthy accounting of why he had not been healed.

"Sir," he says, *"I have no one when the water is moving to put me into the water: but while I am trying to come [into it] myself, someone else steps down ahead of me."* *(Annotated)*

Interestingly enough, while the man's response is hard to understand, close examination reveals some things that help explain a less than enthusiastic response.

To begin, his reply corresponds to a type of response known as "Yes, but."

Research in the field of communication demonstrates that when questions best answered by a simple "Yes" or "No" are answered in another way (such as not answering the question asked or changing the subject) there is reason to suspect some form of conflict (or darkness) in the respondent.

Apparently the disappointment of coming to the pool for years without being healed had taken its toll on the man's spirit as extended physical difficulties tend to do, so much so that he now resists the very thing for which he comes each day.

◆    ◆    ◆

Put yourself in the shoes of the man and walk through the following scenario.

You have come to this same pool for thirty-eight years hoping to be healed.

How many times have the waters been troubled in those years?

How often have you seen your chances for healing evaporate because you were unable to get into the pool when the waters were stirred because those who brought you had returned to their homes or places of business?

Supposing, that on occasion, those who brought you were still at the pool when the waters were stirred, yet, because they had not been able to get you into the pool ahead of everyone else, healing again eluded you.

In short, how many opportunities for healing have been lost?

◆    ◆    ◆

Darkness in the life of the man at the pool takes the form of resistance to Jesus' question.

It is difficult to help individuals who resist the very thing they say they want or need. When counselors encounter resistance in clients they must find ways of cutting through it if they are to be helpful.

Using the power of God, Jesus cuts through resistance in the man and heals him before directing him to take up his bed and walk.

Healing of the lame man reveals darkness in the religious leaders gathered at the pool; darkness that does not permit them to rejoice that a man who had not moved about under his own power for thirty-eight years can walk, in fact, carry his bed. When in their minds the light of healing was weighed against keeping the law, keeping the law was more important.

In the minds of these religious leaders, healing brought darkness to the man's life because it prompted him to do one of thirty-nine things Jewish oral law said was not to be done on the Sabbath, namely, carry a burden.

When used to bring the man to the pool, the bed on which he lay was considered a conveyance. Once he had been healed, however, the bed became a burden. To carry a burden on the Sabbath was work. To work on the Sabbath was a violation of Sabbath law.

◆     ◆     ◆

## A Second Example of Darkness
### (John Chapter Nine)

There is a tendency among human beings to think things should be a certain way, and when they are not that way, to suppose something is wrong, that someone is to blame or that someone has sinned.

Jesus has been teaching in the treasury area of the Temple. In the aftermath of refusing to pass judgment on a woman whom the Scribes and Pharisees allege had been caught in the very act of adultery and an extended dispute as to His identity and the authority with which He speaks, He leaves the area to avoid being stoned by the religious leaders.

Shortly afterward, He encounters a blind man soliciting alms from the people.

Blindness being one of those things that should not be, the disciples are prompted to think someone had sinned. *"Who sinned,"* they ask, *"that he should be born blind?"* (Annotated)

The question posed by the disciples is in keeping with conventional thinking of the First Century according to which righteous men were rewarded with prosperity while wicked men were punished with adversity.

Jesus' response makes it clear that neither the man nor his parents had sinned. The man had simply been born blind that his sightlessness might be used to establish Him as the light of the world in the minds of the people.

Alluding to the "day" as the time allotted for carrying out His mission on earth, and the "night" as the time when He would no longer be able to work, Jesus makes clay, anoints the eyes of the man, and tells him to *"Go, wash in the pool of Siloam—which means sent."*

◆　　◆　　◆

Upon doing as instructed, the man is healed, whereupon, he returns to his home where he encounters darkness in some his neighbors, friends, and the Pharisees.

*"Isn't this the same man who used to sit and beg?"* his neighbors ask.

In contrast to the Pharisees who wanted to know "who opened his eyes," his neighbors want to know "how it was done."

The man to whom sight has been given brings the "who" and the "how" of his healing together by saying, *"The man they call Jesus made mud and put it on my eyes and told me to go to Siloam and wash. So I went and washed, and then I could see."* (NIV)

◆　　◆　　◆

Healing of the man born blind divides the Pharisees into those who claim anyone who broke the Sabbath was a sinner (a sinner defined as one who does not keep the Sabbath), and those who question how a sinner could do such things as give sight to men.

Unwilling to accept that blindness has been replaced by the light of sight, the Jewish leaders question the man's parents hoping to confirm their suspicion that he had not been blind since birth.

Fearing expulsion from the synagogue, the parents identify the man who had received sight as their son, but disclaim knowing who had healed him or anything of how he had been healed. Being of age, their son could speak for himself.

So, exercising their authority the Pharisees recall the man whom Jesus has given sight hoping to pressure him into agreeing with their condemnation of Him as a sinner.

He is told to give God (rather than Jesus) praise for his healing, which is another way of saying, "Tell the truth. Remember you are in God's presence and speak as you would speak to Him."

However, the man stands firm. As far as he is concerned, it doesn't matter who had given him sight or how it had been done. Whether Jesus be saint or sinner, of one thing he is certain, *"I was blind but now I see."*

Summoned a second time, he infuriates the Pharisees to such an extent that they accuse him of being a disciple of Jesus and then shut him out of the synagogue.

While we are not told what transpired following the expulsion of the man from the synagogue, it is possible that if within thirty days he not agreed that Jesus was a sinner, he could have been shut out of the synagogue a second time, this time considered a sinner and a curse or woe pronounced upon him.

Be that as it may, furious that a sinner (in their eyes blindness proved the man a sinner) should presume to instruct people devoted to the study of the Law, the Pharisees hurl insults at the man, quote their authority (Moses) against Jesus (the man's authority), cast him from the synagogue, and excommunicate him which means he was excluded from the community.

Meanwhile, hearing what has happened, Jesus seeks him out and asks, *"Do you believe in the Son of Man?"* the essence of the question being, "Do you believe Jesus to be the source by which the light has come to your life?"

The man believes and acting on the light that has come to his life, worships Jesus.

◆     ◆     ◆

## An Example of Spiritual Darkness
### (John Chapter Three)

The Third Chapter of John finds Nicodemus, a wealthy, well-educated Pharisee, and a member of the Sanhedrin in Jerusalem to observe Passover, the first of three annual feasts requiring the presence of all Jewish males who were sons of Judgment.

Passover being a weeklong observance, Nicodemus had witnessed an undisclosed number of signs and wonders performed by Jesus. These experiences had made a strong impression on him and there was something in what he had witnessed that created a desire to want to know more.

Convinced that in Jesus of Nazareth he would find what he was searching for, Nicodemus seeks an audience. Aware that such a meeting would weaken his influence in the Sanhedrin, the meeting takes place at night, a fact has led some to suppose that it took place in the Garden of Gethsemane.

It is important to have an idea as to what prompted Nicodemus to seek an audience with Jesus. He would, of course, have known Jesus as the leader of a new movement and seems to have concluded that this movement was from God.

Then, too, Jesus' use of the power of God to do things the people believed only God or one sent from God could do must have made a strong impression upon him.

Addressing Jesus as "Rabbi," Nicodemus begins his quest for light. *"We know and are certain that you are a teacher come from God. Obviously no one could show the Signs that you show unless God were with him."* (Phillips *Gospels*)

Jesus hears the words of Nicodemus as the words of a man in search of meaning and purpose to fill the void in his life and so He speaks to him of a "new birth." *"Believe me, no one can even see the Kingdom of God unless he is born again."* (Phillips *Gospels*)

If the only way of filling the void in his life was to be born again, and re-entry into the womb of his Mother a physical impossibility, what Nicodemus faced was a continuing lack of meaning, purpose, and direction in his life.

Even if by some miracle Nicodemus could have entered the womb of his Mother a second time, upon being born he would have been no nearer the Kingdom of God than before because that birth would have been a physical birth.

Being born of the spirit on the other hand made him a disciple and citizen of the Kingdom of God in which men find meaning, purpose, and direction for their lives.

John does not follow Nicodemus beyond this point, therefore, we are not told what his response was to Jesus that night, but tradition has it that Nicodemus became a follower of Christ and was baptized.

Nicodemus appears two additional times in Scripture, once showing great courage by defending Jesus against his colleagues in the Sanhedrin who are bent upon denouncing Jesus as a false prophet and lastly, purchasing spices to be used in the body of Jesus.

One thing is for certain. Nicodemus had meaning, purpose, and direction for his life. In the Kingdom of God he found a "why" for his life.

# 7

# *WHERE THERE IS SADNESS LET ME SOW JOY*

*"...by sadness of countenance the heart is made glad."*

*—Ecclesiastes 7:3*

Having prayed to sow love, pardon, faith, hope, light and joy where hatred, injury, doubt, despair, darkness and sadness is found, St. Francis concluded his prayer petitioning the Lord that he might sow joy where sadness was found.

Sadness is the common denominator in a number of experiences ranging from disappointment and discouragement, unhappiness and depression, to sorrow and loss.

◆     ◆     ◆

Sadness plays a prominent role in three accounts found in the Gospels of the New Testament.

The first is found in a section of the Sermon on the Mount in which Jesus addresses the issue of the spirit in which men are to perform their religious acts.

*"Take care not to do your good deeds publicly or [perform your acts of piety] before men in order to be seen by them."* (Annotated)

Calling attention to one's self when performing a religious act is ostentation, a form of religious dishonesty (or darkness) designed to give the impression that one is devout.

The proper spirit in which men are to perform acts of piety is to perform them in secret, that is, without calling attention to what one is doing. Display or pre-

54

tense makes a sham of religious acts because they shift the focus from the One who is worshiped to the one who is worshiping.

Jesus labeled as hypocrites people who pretended to be religious. He compared making a show of one's piety to cleaning the outside of a cup or platter leaving the inside dirty.

He concluded the Parable of the Pharisee and the Publican by declaring that everyone who exalts himself in the performance of their acts of piety (performing their religious acts to be seen by others) will be humbled, and he who humbles himself by performing his religious acts in secret by refusing to call attention to themselves will be exalted.

◆　　　◆　　　◆

Jesus specifically warned against making a display of giving alms, offering prayers, and fasting. In each instance the sadness present is reflected in the attitudes and on the countenances of men.

"*When you give to the needy,*" He said, "*do not announce it with trumpets as the hypocrites do in the synagogues and on the streets, to be honored by men* [to be seen of them]." (NIV)

"*When you pray do not be like the play actors. They love to stand and pray in the synagogues and at street corners so that people may see them at it.*" (Phillips *Gospels*)

It is with regard to fasting, however, that sadness in a religious act is most evident.

Jesus said, "*Do not look gloomy and sour and dreary like the hypocrites, for they put on a dismal countenance, that their fasting may be apparent to and seen by men.*" (Annotated)

In the time of Jesus, people fasted for a variety of reasons, sometimes out of necessity because of a shortage of food, at other times because fasting made them more sensitive to God's spirit, especially, when seeking His Will and direction.

Whether public or private, however, fasting is intended to be a joyful experience. Therefore, as men are to avoid calling attention to what they are doing when giving to the needy and offering their prayers, those who fast are to avoid the appearance of sadness by washing their faces.

While an outward display of piety may make one look good in the eyes of a neighbor, it does nothing to change the hearts of people. Pretence never does.

The reward of those who wear sad, disfigured faces when fasting is to be seen of men while the reward of those for whom fasting is an genuine act of worship is the satisfaction of knowing they will be rewarded by their Heavenly Father.

◆     ◆     ◆

A second account in which sadness is present takes place on the afternoon of resurrection day on the road from Jerusalem to Emmaus (24:13-31).

Having been in Jerusalem during the week prior to the crucifixion of Jesus, most likely to observe the Feast of Passover commemorating the Exodus of the Hebrew people from Egypt, Cleopas and a companion are returning to their homes in the city of Emmaus.

Luke's reference to the look on the faces of these men as sad and downcast, and the hint that their conversation was so rapid that they appeared to be throwing words at each other suggests the topics being discussed were extremely important and the desire to understand the things that had happened so strong that the two were oblivious of everything around them, thus, when Jesus joins them and asks, *"What is it that you are discussing as you walk along?"* they were startled and frightened. (Annotated)

As they walked the two men had been rehearsing what had happened in Jerusalem from Jesus' entry into the city the previous week to that very morning when women had gone to the tomb of Joseph of Arimathea and found it empty.

Like others of the time, they seem not to have understood who Jesus was, that He was Messiah, the kind of king whose purpose was to fulfill rather than overthrow, or that His was a spiritual kingdom placed in the innermost part of men in which greatness is measured in terms of service rather than in positions held and power wielded.

◆     ◆     ◆

*"Are you only a visitor to Jerusalem and do not know the things that have happened there?"* asks Cleopas, suggesting he and his companion found it inconceivable that anyone could have been in the city and yet unaware of the things that had happened. (Annotated)

Had Jesus been a resident, He would have been aware of the entrance of the man from Galilee and may have been a part of the crowd that accompanied Him into the city singing praises to God.

Jerusalem being within the jurisdiction of the Sanhedrin, even visitors to the city would have been aware that after entering the city Jesus had been taken to Caiaphas the high priest and later delivered to Pilate who, fearing a riot might ensue, declared himself innocent of Jesus' blood, symbolically absolving himself from culpability in what was about to happen by washing his hands prior to delivering Jesus to be crucified.

*"And what is more,"* continues Cleopas, *"Jesus had said He would rise on the third day."*

The men were sad, in part, because they considered Jesus to be a prophet, perhaps the one they had been looking for who would redeem Israel, and perhaps by the knowledge that some women had gone to the tomb early that morning and found it empty.

Having listened to their words, Jesus invites the two startled, frightened disciples to touch him that they might know He is flesh and blood and not a ghost.

Still, they are unable to believe who He is, prompting Jesus to remark, *"How foolish you are, and how slow of heart to believe all that the prophets have spoken."* *(Annotated)*

Jesus was not calling the two men fools. He was simply acknowledging they lacked the capacity to discern the meaning of His suffering, death, and resurrection, and to correctly identify who He was.

So, beginning with Moses and all the prophets, Jesus explains what was said in the Scriptures concerning Himself.

◆     ◆     ◆

Assuming Jesus had joined Cleopas and his friend in the vicinity of Jerusalem, the distance to Emmaus being seven miles suggests conversation with the two disciples could have lasted as long as two hours.

By now it is late afternoon, the time when travelers would ordinarily begin exercising the right that was theirs to seek lodging for the night.

There would be no need for Jesus to exercise this right for Cleopas and his companion invite Him to accept the hospital of their city.

Later that evening, Jesus shares a meal with the two men similar to His last meal with the disciples in Jerusalem.

◆     ◆     ◆

It is interesting to compare the meal eaten with the disciples in Jerusalem and the post resurrection meal eaten with Cleopas and his friend at Emmaus.

The two meals are similar with respect to why they were eaten and the procedure followed in eating them.

The meal at Emmaus, like the one eaten in Jerusalem was motivated by Jesus' desire to demonstrate love for men who were His disciples, His need to model for His followers the way they were to remember Him, and His hope that such a meal would bind the disciples to Himself and to each other.

◆     ◆     ◆

It should be noted that prior to leaving on an extended journey that it was customary for men of the First Century to demonstrate love for friends and acquaintances by eating a meal with them. The procedure for eating a meal of this kind was well established in the culture of the people.

First, the host at this kind of meal would give food to his guests. As the host of the meal in Jerusalem, Jesus had given bread to the disciples and after offering thanks had told them, *"Take eat, this is my body."*

One can only assume Jesus followed the same procedure in Emmaus.

Regardless of how far the journey of the host might take him from men he loved food eaten at such a meal would symbolize his body to them.

Having given food to his guests the host would then give them wine with instructions to drink. In Jerusalem Jesus had taken the cup and offering it to the disciples, said, *"This is my blood of the covenant, which is poured out for many for the forgiveness of sins."* (RSV)

Just as food symbolized the body of the host, wine symbolized his life.

In the relational acts of breaking bread and drinking wine, hosts said to their guests, "Regardless of how far my journey may take me, though we be removed from each other by great distances, I am always with you! Be at peace."

At Emmaus, Jesus does not give wine to Cleopas and his friend for after giving them the bread, their eyes are opened, they recognize who he is, and then He is gone out of their sight.

◆     ◆     ◆

The third, and final reference to sadness is a part of Jesus' encounter with a rich, young man in the Nineteenth Chapter of Matthew's Gospel (19:16-26).

Disregarding whether the person in question was young or as some think, middle age (because the word translated "young" can refer to anyone beyond the teen years to someone in their early forties), what he sought was the spiritual reality of eternal life, and so he asks, *"What must I do to have eternal life?"*

*"Obey the commandments,"* is the reply Jesus makes before proceeding to name the commandments relating to man's duty to his neighbor.

Having lived an exemplary life, the young man responds, *"All these I have kept,"* [all the commandments Jesus had named] he replies, *"What do I still lack?"* (Annotated)

While his life may have indeed been exemplary, to move beyond where he was, or in Jesus' words, *"to be perfect,"* would require that he sell his possessions and give the money to the poor.

What Jesus did by directing the young man to sell his goods and give the proceeds to the poor was suggest to him that he lacked compassion for his fellow man.

But he could not. Instead, Matthew says, *"the young man went away sad, because he had great wealth."* He would not have what he desired.

◆      ◆      ◆

In the last sentence of his prayer, St. Francis prayed to sow joy where sadness was found.

Joy, the antidote to sadness, has been described as the pleasure men feel in the innermost part of their being when they think of a present or future good. In words of a song children sing in Sunday School, *"I've got the joy, joy, joy, joy down in my heart."*

◆      ◆      ◆

Basically, joy is a derivative of love.

Earlier two understandings of love were presented: love understood as feeling and love understood as a commitment.

Having commented upon the shortcomings of the former and noted the merits of the latter, only love understood as commitment seems capable of producing joy.

This being the case how are instruments of peace to apply the antidote of joy in such a way that sadness fades?

◆        ◆        ◆

Instruments of peace apply the antidote of joy by committing themselves to meeting the needs and acting in the best interest of those in whom sadness is present.

What this suggests is that joy is produced when we commit our wills to loving people (ourselves and others) the way Jesus has commanded, meeting our own needs and those of others, acting in our own best interests and the best interests of others, and addressing the concerns of everyone involved.

Broadly understood a "need" is something humans cannot do without for very long, or which cannot remain unmet for an extended period without our experiencing lowered self-esteem and a sense of well being.

A concern, by contrast, is something that commands the attention of men. While they may think about it and, perhaps, talk it over with others, they may never act upon it.

As men everywhere have needs and concerns, to overcome sadness instruments of peace must sow joy in the lives of others with the same dedication Jesus said men were to love, with all their heart, with all their soul, and with all their might.

Yet, in a society where love is understood primarily as feeling, whose value system has been altered radically by social forces, in which religion is increasingly removed from public life, joy has become something of an illusion.

Just as it is an illusion to think the world is a safe place, that the world is fair and just, and that someone will always be there for us, it is an illusion to suppose joy can be found in anything external to ourselves. Joy is found only in love.

George Bernard Shaw once described joy as *"being used for a purpose recognized by yourself as a mighty one* [what Wilfred Grenfell called a worthwhile purpose], *the being thoroughly worn out before you are thrown on the scrap heap; the being a force of nature instead of a feverish selfish little clod of ailments and grievances complaining that the world will not devote itself to making you happy."*[3]

Theologically, joy is a quality of life when God's love is present. Because joy is a derivative or by-product of love, where God's love is present joy will be present as well. There is no joy, however, where things are loved and people are used, where things are prized more highly than people.

Psychologically, joy is an index or measure of how one feels about life in general and his or her life in particular.

Men and women able to esteem and present the image they have of themselves experience joy more readily than others because they are at peace in the innermost part of their being. Men at peace in the depths of their being look on the bright side of things, view people in a positive light, and put the best possible interpretation upon what happens to them.

Approaching life joyfully the needs of people are met in the relationships they establish, the kind of aloneness God saw was not good for men is avoided, and they have the kind of experiences they yearn for in relation to individuals emotionally significant to them.

◆    ◆    ◆

It has been said that joy comes in many packages.

When it is one's nature to be loving joy is packed as cheerfulness.

When goals are attained and objectives reached joy comes packaged as gladness and satisfaction.

When one can say, "It's okay to be where I am" joy comes packaged as contentment.

In addition, joy comes packaged in the beauty of a sunset, music, art, the skill of a performer, a task well done or, relationship with someone emotionally significant to us.

Writers of the Old Testament, especially, the Psalmists, packaged joy in expressions like the one that introduces the First Psalm.

"*Blessed is the man*" writes the Psalmist before identifying as happy and joyful the man who does not accept the advice or plans of sinners, nor sits with them in their deliberations because his delight is to fulfill the law.

◆    ◆    ◆

In the New Testament joy is what men feel when blessed for having acquired traits and characteristics God desires in disciples and citizens of the Kingdom of God.

Accordingly, joy comes in

• detaching from earth and things of earth and placing one's trust in God

• responding to the circumstances of one's neighbors bringing comfort and assurance to those walking through the Valley of Dark Shadows in the wake of the severing of ties with individuals emotionally significant to them.

Joy also comes in

- the acquisition of strength of character that merits the good things of earth summed up in the Kingdom of God, and

- being filled with the righteousness for which men hunger and thirst.

In addition, joy comes in

- showing mercy and compassion to neighbors by becoming actively involved in the lives of those whose circumstances are difficult and whose situations are trying, and

- in bringing wholeness, contentment, tranquility, and fulfillment to lives plagued by fear and hatred, loneliness and hunger.

Joy comes as well to those

- whose motives are pure, whose thoughts are unadulterated, whose attitudes are without contamination, and whose behavior is above reproach, and

- in knowing that one's life approximates that of Christ so closely that the world takes notice.

But the greatest joy of all is being honored with the title "Children of God" because one has worked for contentment, fulfillment, and wholeness in the lives of others are honored.

◆     ◆     ◆

While the avenues to joy are numerous, joy can be, and often is, lost. It is lost in the pursuit of philosophies and lifestyles that run counter to the "Thou shalts" and the "Thou shalt nots" of the Ten Commandments.

It vanishes in disappointment, broken commitments, the betrayal of friendship and trust, the refusal of help in times of great need, the severing of ties with persons emotionally significant to us in experiences of loss, and the discounting of oneself as a person of worth and value.

Beyond these things joy is lost when men and nations cease to be true to themselves, their neighbors, and their God.

Israel provides a clear example of how joy is lost.

After four hundred years of servitude to the Pharaohs of Egypt, a liberated Israel journeyed in a generally southeasterly direction toward the Sinai Peninsula.

Upon reaching the Mount of Sinai God made a covenant with the people He had chosen.

Speaking through Moses, Yahweh says, *"You yourselves have seen what I did to Egypt, and how I bare you on eagles' wings and brought you to myself. If you will obey my voice indeed, and keep my covenant, then out of all nations you will be my treasured possession. Although the whole earth is mine, you will be for me a kingdom of priests and a holy nation."* (NIV)

But the record of Israel's keeping of the covenant is a sad commentary on the willingness of humankind to forsake the God who is real to worship gods that are not real. In failing to live up to their responsibilities under the covenant Israel altered the course of its national life and history itself.

With alarming frequency the Old Testament announces, *"And the children of Israel did evil in the sight of God, and forsook Him,"* worshipping gods that could neither speak nor communicate, that had to be carried because they could not walk, gods who were not feared because they could not harm but, regrettably could do no good.

Jeremiah records Israel's loss of joy in words laden with pathos and sadness, *"By the rivers of Babylon, there we [captives] sat down and wept when we remembered Zion [the city of our God imprinted on our hearts]. On the willow trees in the midst of [Babylon] we hung our harps. For there they who led us captive required of us a song with words, and they who wasted us required of us mirth, saying, Sing us one of the songs of Zion."* (Annotated)

♦    ♦    ♦

We are called to be joyful in a world which admittedly has fallen short of God's ideal and intent, a world given to philosophies of life, styles of living, and systems of values that lead us to wonder "Is this all there is?"

We are called to be joyful in a society that worships aggressive behavior, whose ambitions are limitless, in whose life spiritual values have been replaced by external values, a society that ignores the reality that meaning and purpose for life are not found in anything external to oneself.

Be that as it may, joy is something we must have. If it has been lost, it must be recovered.

The question is how?

The composer of the hymn, *"In The Heart He Implanteth a Song,"* suggests joy is recovered in songs of deliverance, courage, and strength.

The song of deliverance is faith. It is faith that delivers us from our sins and assures us God is present in all the experiences of life, whether these are thrust upon us or they come as a result of poor decisions on our part.

The song of courage is hope. Hope speaks with the voice of angels breathing lessons many do not hear. It whispers comforting, reassuring words gently and persuasively. "Wait, it says, "the darkness will not last. The tempest will pass. Hope for the sunshine after the shower is gone." Beyond the Valley of Dark Shadows is a table prepared by God with all the things you need.

The song of strength is love. *"We have every reason to hope,"* wrote Detriech Bonhoffer *to his friend, Eberhard Bethge, "because God's love has been poured into our hearts."*

In the Lord's Prayer one discovers joy comes in hallowing the name of God, in welcoming the Kingdom of God, in the doing of God's will, for while one may be required to walk through the Valley of Dark Shadows the joy of the sheep is that the shepherd is with them.

Assured of these things, the cup of joy fills to overflowing and men experience the joy that comes in knowing that one will dwell in the House of the God of love forever.

# *CONCLUSION*

Francis of Assisi is one of Christianity's most exemplary figures. Humble and fervent, it was his desire to become an instrument of God's peace that he might address conditions that robbed men and women of meaning, purpose, abundance, fulfillment, and direction for their lives.

He understood that for humankind to experience the kind of peace Jesus bestowed upon His disciples that hatred, injury, doubt, despair, darkness, and sadness must be overcome.

◆　　◆　　◆

To overcome hatred he proposed to sow the kind of love that brings meaning, purpose, and direction to the lives of men and women lest hatred lead to strife, conflict, and the use of force with the intent to harm.

Francis had great confidence in love as the remedy for hatred because love is patient and kind, not jealous or boastful, does not exalt itself, is neither arrogant or rude, did not insist on its own way, was neither irritable or resentful or touchy, does not rejoice in wrong, bears all things, believes all things, and endures all things.

◆　　◆　　◆

To overcome injury he proposed remedies of pardon and forgiveness because these enable men and women to rise above what has happened to them and work for healing in their own life and reconciliation between themselves and their offenders lest relationships be fractured beyond the point of being able to meet the needs of individuals as well as those of society.

◆　　◆　　◆

To overcome doubt, he proposed faith certain faith was the substance and evidence of God in the lives of men and women.

◆        ◆        ◆

To overcome despair, he proposed hope, not as a lesser virtue than faith and love, but a remedy that enables men and women to breath prayers that gives scope to their anguish, a virtue enabling men to declare with confidence that all things work together for good to those who love God.

◆        ◆        ◆

To overcome darkness, he proposed light because it is capable of dispelling physical, emotional, and spiritual darkness enabling men to live richer, fuller, more productive lives.

◆        ◆        ◆

To overcome sadness he proposed to sow joy because as a derivative of love joy is what brings meaning to man's innermost being prompting him to give himself in service to the God whose love is the source of joy.

◆        ◆        ◆

To become an instrument of God's peace men and women must believe themselves called to the service of the divine by an inner prompting or vision.

To be effective in their calling they must be at peace with themselves. The spiritual and psychological dimensions of their inner life must be in accord. What they believe must square with how they live.

To bring these dimensions of life into harmony instruments of peace must fashion a self-image they can esteem and present in ways that facilitate connecting with others, and at the same time, encourages others to admit them into their lives.

◆        ◆        ◆

In a lifetime of service to God, St. Francis discovered greatness lies in service to others.

In consoling others servants are consoled. In understanding others they are understood. In loving others they are loved. In giving to others they receive. In pardoning others they are assured of forgiveness. In loving others they are loved. In giving to others they receive. In pardoning others they are pardoned. And in dying to one's self they are born to eternal life.

◆    ◆    ◆

Prayer of an instrument of God's peace.

*"Father, make me an instrument of thy peace that I may show others a more gentle way because life is hard, a more dependable way because the times are uncertain, a quieter way because the world is noisy, a more concerned way because many are indifferent, a more compassionate way because some are uncaring, a more accepting way because of who I am, a more loving way because of who you are."*

# BIBLIOGRAPHY

Blackburn, Bill. *Understanding Your Feelings.* Nashville: Broadman Press, 1983.

Bonhoeffer, Dietrich. *Letters and Papers From Prison.* ed. Eberhard Bethge. New York: Simon and Shuster, 1997.

Callwood, June. *Love, the, Fear, Anger and the Other Lively Emotions.* N.P: Newcastle Publishing Company, 1964.

Hastings, James. *Hastings Dictionary Of The Bible.* 2$^{nd}$ ed. New York: Hendrickson Press, 1994.

Murray, Anne. *The Best of Anne Murray.* CD distributed by Cema Special Markets.

Tillich, Paul. *Dynamics of Faith.* New York: Harper and Brothers, 1957.

Wahlroos, Sven. *Family Communication.* New York: Macmillan Publishing company, 1974.

0-595-27939-2

Printed in the United Kingdom
by Lightning Source UK Ltd.
102651UKS00001B/338

9 780595 279395